Crayola World of GREEN

Mari Schuh

Lerner Publications ◆ Minneapolis

For Dylan and Robbie

Official Licensed Product
Lerner Publications Company
An imprint of Lerner Publishing Group, Inc.
241 First Avenue North
Minneapolis, MN 55401 USA

For reading levels and more information, look up this title at www.lernerbooks.com.

Main body text set in Mikado a Medium 20/28.
Typeface provided by HVD Fonts.

Library of Congress Cataloging-in-Publication Data

Names: Schuh, Mari C., 1975- author. | Crayola (Firm)
Title: The world of green / by Mari Schuh.
Description: Minneapolis : Lerner Publications, [2019] | Series: Crayola world of color | Audience: Age 5–9. | Audience: K to Grade 3. | Includes bibliographical references and index.
Identifiers: LCCN 2018040122 | ISBN 9781541554672 (lb : alk. paper)
Subjects: LCSH: Green—Juvenile literature. | Color in nature—Juvenile literature. | Colors—Juvenile literature. | Crayons—Juvenile literature.
Classification: LCC QC495.5 .S36875 2019 | DDC 535.6—dc23

LC record available at https://lccn.loc.gov/2018040122

Manufactured in the United States of America
1-45785-42667-11/19/2018

CONTENTS

Hello, Green! . . . . (4)

Green in Nature . . . . (6)

Green Animals . . . . (10)

Green Foods . . . . (16)

Green Where You Live . . . . (22)

Color with Green! . . . . (28)

Green All around You . . . . (29)

Glossary   30
To Learn More   31
Index   32

Hello, Green!

Shades of **green** are all around.

Find **teal**, **olive**, **emerald**, **lime**, and **forest green**.
Green is almost everywhere!
Where do you see **green**?

Green in Nature

Green covers the forest trees. Fresh leaves open up for the sun.

Green grows in the hot, dry desert. Sharp spines cover prickly cactuses.

Be careful!

Green Animals

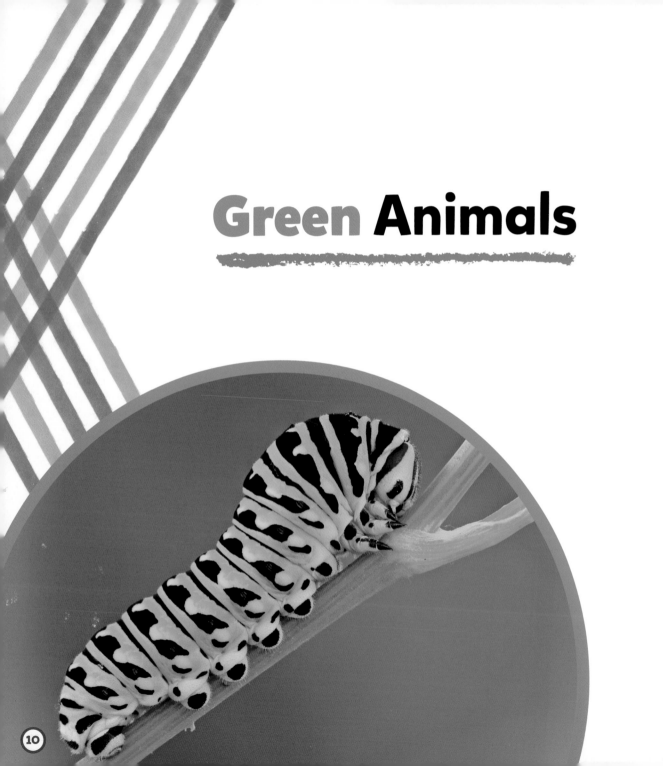

See **green** slither along the ground. Tiny scales protect snakes. Caterpillars munch on leaves.

Green peeks out from the pond.
Water keeps this frog's skin moist.

Ribbit! Ribbit!

Green parrots perch high in the trees. Lots of feathers keep them warm and dry.

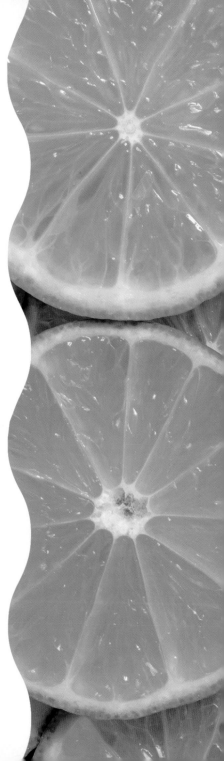

Green **Foods**

Green can be juicy. Apples, kiwis, and limes are tasty and good for you. Take a bite!

Green grows in the sun. Fill your plate with leafy lettuce. Nibble on plump **green** grapes.

Yum!

Ice cream, mints, and candies.
Green can be a special treat!
Which one is your favorite?

Green Where You Live

Green means go! It helps people on the move. Where will you go next?

You can find **green** where you play. Slide, bike, and climb. Have all sorts of fun with **green**!

Green is busy! Big machines work in the fields. Cars and buses zoom around town.

Where else can you find **green**?

Color with Green!

Draw a picture using only **green** crayons. What will you draw? What shades of **green** will you use?

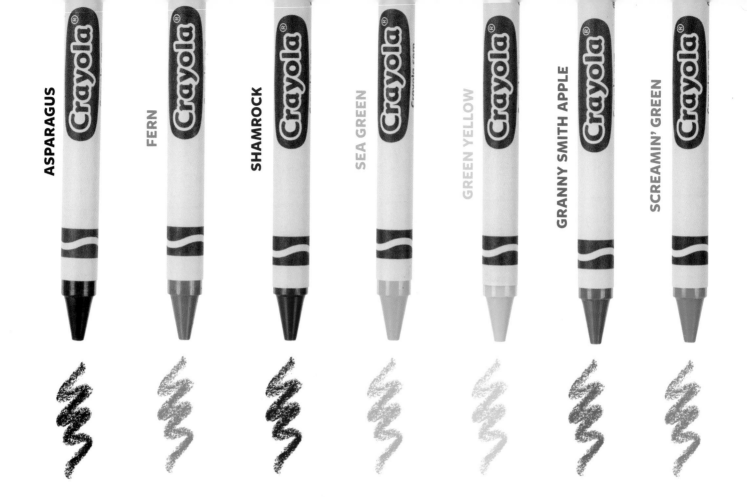

ASPARAGUS

FERN

SHAMROCK

SEA GREEN

GREEN YELLOW

GRANNY SMITH APPLE

SCREAMIN' GREEN

Green All around You

Green is everywhere. Here are some Crayola® crayon shades of **green** used in this book. Can you find all of them in the photos? What's your favorite shade of **green**?

Glossary

kiwi: a small fruit with green flesh and brown skin

moist: slightly wet

perch: to stand on the edge of a branch or other object

scale: a small, hard plate that covers a snake's body

shade: the lightness or darkness of a color

slither: to slide and move along the ground

spine: a sharp, pointy part of a plant or animal

To Learn More

Books

Leaf, Christina. *Green Animals*. Minneapolis: Bellwether Media, 2019.
Explore the color green by reading about green animals.

Shepherd, Jodie. *Crayola Spring Colors*. Minneapolis: Lerner Publications, 2018.
Read about all the colors you can find during spring, including the color green!

Websites

Crayola Coloring Page: Camping Search and Find
http://www.crayola.com/free-coloring-pages/print/camping-search-and-find
-coloring-page/
Color a camping scene with green snakes and big, green trees.

Kid Zone: Green Coloring Page
http://www.kidzone.ws/prek_wrksht/colors/colors-green1.htm
Use your green crayons to color green objects.

Index

buses, 27

cactuses, 9

frogs, 13

grapes, 19

kiwis, 17

leaves, 7
limes, 5, 17

parrots, 14

snakes, 11

treats, 21

Photo Acknowledgments

Image credits: ArTDi101/Shutterstock.com, pp. 2, 6 (leaves); Smileus/Shutterstock.com, p. 4 (grass); languste/Shutterstock.com, p. 4 (chameleon); graja/Shutterstock.com, p. 5 (ice-cream bar); Elena Larina/Shutterstock.com, p. 5 (peas); VikaLugano/Shutterstock.com, p. 5 (flowers); vovan/Shutterstock.com, pp. 6–7 (forest); janniwet/Shutterstock.com, pp. 8–9; Tyler Fox/Shutterstock.com, p. 10 (larva); arwenhuang/Shutterstock.com, pp. 10–11 (snake); Michael Steden/Shutterstock.com, pp. 12–13; cuatrok77/Flickr (CC BY-SA 2.0), pp. 14–15; Elena11/Shutterstock.com, p. 16 (kiwi); yuratosno3/Shutterstock.com, pp. 16–17 (limes); grey_and/Shutterstock.com, p. 17 (apples); goodgold99/Shutterstock.com, pp. 18–19 (garden); Tim UR/Shutterstock.com, p. 19 (grapes); Africa Studio/Shutterstock.com, pp. 20–21; JR T/Shutterstock.com, p. 21 (peppermint candy); Douglas Johns/StockFood Creative/Getty Images, p. 21 (ice cream cone); IZZ HAZEL/Shutterstock.com, p. 22 (traffic light); Ken Wolter/Shutterstock.com, pp. 22–23 (bikes); Sergiy1975/Shutterstock.com, pp. 24–25; smereka/Shutterstock.com, pp. 26–27 (combine); Michael Shake/Shutterstock.com, p. 27 (car); zorina_larisa/Shutterstock.com (design elements throughout).

Cover: Timolina/Shutterstock.com (peas); Boule/Shutterstock.com (frog); YewLoon Lam/Shutterstock.com (snake); KAE CH/Shutterstock.com (leaves).